Pat Sloan's
I CAN'T BELIEVE I'M
QUILTING

DEAR READER,

YOU MAY WONDER WHAT INSPIRED ME TO CREATE A BOOK FOR BEGINNING QUILTERS. MY REASONING IS SIMPLE — NOT SO VERY LONG AGO, I WAS IN YOUR SHOES.

You see, I've had a love affair with cloth and textiles for a very long time. I've sewn since I was a little girl, often making doll clothing by hand, but I had never even seen a quilt until I met my future in-laws. Both of my husband's grandmothers made simple utility bed quilts, perfect for keeping warm in the cold Pennsylvania winters. They recycled fabric from worn-out clothing and sheets, turning them into cozy quilts.

When my husband, Gregg, and I got our first apartment in the late 1970's, I made a quilt. I bought a magazine, some fabric, a sheet for the back, (it was big enough!) and then tied the quilt with yarn like Gregg's grandmothers did. But after completing this project, I set down the quilting needle for several years in favor of sewing clothing.

Then, in 1992, my friend Gwyn decided I needed to learn to quilt. She took me to a quilt shop and signed me up for a five-week class. By the end of the first class I had the quilting bug big time! Since then, quilting has become my favorite pastime, and I feel both excited and privileged to share the basics of this wonderful hobby with you.

You are about to go on an incredible journey of discovery. This book includes easy-to-follow instructions that will teach you to quilt by hand the way our grandmothers and their grandmothers did — a portable, fun, and relaxing form of handwork! Or, if you prefer, follow the tips on machine quilting and rotary cutting to finish your quilts more quickly.

I've designed this book to be very friendly, with a series of small projects you can start and complete. My quilts are fun and fast, intended to build your skills while you successfully finish projects. For best results, I recommend following the book from beginning to end, fine-tuning your skills on the easier projects before you take on the more difficult ones.

I wish you all the best of luck as you explore this exciting craft, and I hope you love it as much as I do.

HAPPY QUILTING!
Pat Sloan

MEET THE *Designer*

FOR DESIGNER *Pat Sloan*, QUILTING HAS "SHAPED UP" INTO AN OCCUPATION SHE NEVER WOULD HAVE DREAMED OF PURSUING.

Although Pat grew up sewing and crafting, she didn't dive into the world of quilting until 1992. "At first I thought it would be boring," Pat admits, "but a friend signed me up, and I haven't looked back."

Since then, quilting has become Pat's favorite activity, in part because she enjoys working with her hands. "I like that motion, the action of creating something, especially with fabric," she says. "I've tried all the crafts … and cloth is my favorite."

This enthusiasm for quilting led Pat, a former computer programmer who worked in human resources, to quit her job in the late 1990s. "I just had to find a way to quilt full-time," Pat says. "I started designing because I had to choose something that I could develop very quickly."

Pat admits that she was actually very nervous at the thought of quitting her job. "I'm conservative — I'd never done anything like that before!" she confesses. But her husband, Gregg, gave her the extra encouragement she needed, telling her to "just go for it." And as the business has grown, Gregg has continued to support Pat by quitting his own job to work full-time at Pat Sloan & Co, which designs and publishes patterns for quilts, penny rugs, and rug hooking. "He does all the printing, editing, shipping … everything but color and design!" Pat laughs.

Design has indeed remained Pat's domain, and the ideas seem to flow naturally from the converted living room where she spends most of her working day. Her style tends toward old-fashioned, yet whimsical, quilts and wall hangings — not surprising since she finds much of her inspiration in old Baltimore appliqué quilts, which she feels have "lots of personality."

Pat currently divides her time between designing, managing her company, and teaching workshops and seminars on quilting (about 10 per year). She hopes to teach more classes in the future, as well as develop more books. Recently Pat designed her first line of fabrics, "Old Blooms," which is being produced by P&B Textiles.

When asked what she attributes her success to, Pat responds, "I believed I could do it … I enjoy what I do, and hopefully other people enjoy it, too."

THE PROJECTS IN THIS BOOK ARE DESIGNED TO BE EASY, FAST, AND INTRODUCE YOU TO THE BASICS OF QUILTMAKING. While each project does include complete instructions and it is not necessary to begin with Lesson 1, you may find it helpful to begin with this easy project and work your way up to the more difficult project in Lesson 6. Each Lesson is designed to reinforce techniques you have learned in previous lessons and introduce you to new ones.

ANATOMY OF A QUILT

When we think of quilts, our grandmother's bed coverings usually come to mind. Today's quilts are made to serve a variety of uses including bed coverings, wall hangings, table coverings, tote bags, and clothing. Just about anything that can be made of fabric can be quilted.

A quilt is unique because it consists of 2 layers of fabric (quilt top and backing) with a filler material (batting) sandwiched in between. The layers are stitched together, usually in a decorative manner (quilting), to keep them from shifting during use.

DECISION TIME

Before you begin, you will have some decisions to make about the different techniques you can use when making a quilt. Choose between the following techniques.

Template Cutting or Rotary Cutting

Hand Piecing or Machine Piecing

Hand Quilting or Machine Quilting

Template cutting, hand piecing and hand quilting are the traditional methods used by quilters for centuries. Hand piecing and hand quilting projects are very portable allowing you to work on them virtually anywhere. Hand piecing allows for greater control and produces soft seams which can easily be pressed in any direction. Piecing and quilting by hand, however, can be very time consuming.

Rotary cutting, machine piecing and machine quilting are modern techniques, which have brought speed and accuracy to the quilt-making process. Machine sewing allows for a stronger stitch, helpful for projects that will receive heavy use and frequent washings.

You may choose to use a combination of methods. Template or rotary cutting can be used with any piecing or quilting technique. Some quilters like to machine piece and hand quilt while others prefer to hand piece and machine quilt. Some choose to piece and quilt only by hand or only by machine.

Carefully read the **Cutting**, **Piecing and Pressing**, and **Quilting** sections to help you decide which methods appeal to you the most. Keep in mind how quickly you want to finish a project, the size of your project, and whether you enjoy hand or machine work. Remember, there are no right or wrong choices; it is simply a matter of personal preference. Once you have decided on the techniques you will use, refer to **Tools and Supplies** to select the specific tools you will need to complete your project.

Quilting Terms

LEARNING TO SPEAK "QUILTISH"

While quilter's do not have a language all their own, some terms may seem foreign to a novice, so we have included a list of frequently used quilting terms.

Backing – The bottom layer of a quilt.

Backstitch – A reinforcing stitch taken at the beginning and end of a seam to secure stitches.

Basting – Large running stitches used to temporarily secure pieces or layers of fabric together. Basting is removed after permanent stitching.

Batting – The middle layer of a quilt that provides the insulation and warmth as well as the thickness.

Bias – The diagonal (45° for true bias) grain of fabric in relation to crosswise or lengthwise grain (see **Fig. 1**).

Binding – The fabric strip used to enclose the raw edges of the layered and quilted quilt. Also refers to the technique of finishing quilt edges in this way.

Border – Strips of fabric that are used to frame a quilt top.

Chain piecing – A machine-piecing method consisting of joining pairs of pieces one after the other by feeding them through the sewing machine without cutting the thread between the pairs.

Finger press – A technique used to make seam allowances lie flat by smoothing a seam with your finger or a wooden hand tool. Most often used when hand piecing.

Grain – The direction of the threads in woven fabric. "Crosswise grain" refers to the threads running from selvage to selvage. "Lengthwise grain" refers to the threads running parallel to the selvages (**Fig. 1**).

Fig. 1

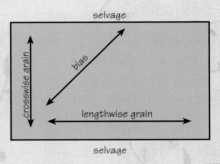

Machine baste – To baste using a sewing machine set at a long stitch length.

Piecing – Sewing together the pieces of a quilt top to form a quilt block or an entire quilt top.

Pin basting – Using rustproof safety pins to secure the layers of a quilt together prior to machine quilting.

Quilt blocks – Pieced sections that are sewn together to form a quilt top.

Quilt top – The decorative part of a quilt that is layered on top of the batting and backing.

Quilting — The stitching that holds together the 3 quilt layers (top, batting, and backing); or, the entire process of making a quilt.

Quilting lines — Designs drawn on fabric with a marking tool. Quilting lines are used as a guide when quilting.

Running stitch — A series of straight stitches with the stitch length equal to the space between the stitches.

Sashing — Strips of fabric that separate individual blocks in a quilt top.

Seam — The line of stitches formed when sewing 2 pieces of fabric together.

Seam allowance — The distance between the seam and the cut edge of the fabric. In quilting, the seam allowance is usually $1/4$".

Selvages — The 2 tightly woven lengthwise edges of fabric.

Set or Setting — The arrangement of the quilt blocks as they are sewn together to form the quilt top.

Setting squares — Squares of plain (unpieced) fabric set between pieced blocks in a quilt top.

Stencil — A pattern used for marking quilting lines.

Straight grain — The crosswise or lengthwise grain of fabric (see **Fig. 1**). The lengthwise grain has the least amount of stretch.

Strip set — Two or more strips of fabric that are sewn together along the long edges and then cut apart across the width of the sewn strips to create smaller units.

Template — A pattern made of sturdy material (we suggest template plastic). Templates are placed on the fabric, then a marking tool is used to draw around the template directly onto the fabric.

Triangle-square — 2 right triangles joined along their long sides to form a square with a diagonal seam.

Unit — Fabric pieces sewn together to form subgroups. Units are usually combined to make blocks or other sections of the quilt top.

Walking Foot — A sewing machine presser foot that feeds two or more layers of fabric evenly as you quilt. Sometimes it is referred to as an even-feed foot.

WOULD YOU CUT DOWN A TREE WITH A BUTTER KNIFE?

Whether you are cutting, piecing, or quilting, using the right tools and supplies will make the process easier and more enjoyable. Our list contains all of the basic supplies needed to complete the projects in this book. When you move on to more advanced projects, check out other specialty tools available to add to your basic supplies.

TEMPLATE CUTTING

Fabric scissors – Good quality 8" dressmaker shears sharp enough to cut through several layers of fabric. Save these for fabric cutting only.

Utility scissors – General purpose scissors for cutting paper and template plastic.

Template plastic – Sheets of translucent plastic used for making templates and quilting stencils. Some template plastic has a 1/4" grid for ease in cutting.

Fabric marking pencils – Three types of pencils are useful; a mechanical pencil with 0.5 mm soft or medium lead such as B or HB for marking fabric or drawing on paper, a Quilter's silver pencil for marking on light or dark fabrics, and a white chalk pencil for marking dark fabrics.

Fine-point permanent marker – For tracing patterns onto template plastic.

Sandpaper – Placing a sheet of extra-fine sandpaper under your fabric will help prevent fabric from shifting when drawing around templates.

Ruler – 3" x 18" long acrylic ruler with 1/8" markings to use when tracing patterns is useful but any ruler will work.

ROTARY CUTTING

Cutting mat — A self-healing plastic mat with 1" grid lines designed to be used with a rotary cutter. 18" x 24" or larger is recommended.

Rotary cutting rulers — A thick clear acrylic ruler with $1/8$" crosswise and lengthwise markings and markings for 30°, 45° and 60° angles. While these rulers are available in a large range of sizes, we recommend purchasing a 3" x 18", 6" x 24", and a square $12^1/2$" or larger. Later you may wish to add other sizes.

Rotary cutter — A cutting tool made up of a sharp, round blade mounted on a handle used to cut fabric. Several styles and sizes are available. We suggest one with a 45 mm blade. If possible, hold and try different ones to find the one you are most comfortable with. Always use with a cutting mat and acrylic ruler.

Fabric scissors — See Template Cutting.

HAND PIECING

Needles — Sharp, thin all-purpose needles called "Sharps" are used for hand piecing. Try different sizes ranging from 8 to 12 until you find the one that is most comfortable for you.

Thimble — A thimble should fit securely on the middle finger of your sewing hand. Metal thimbles with a flat top and deep dimples help keep the needle from slipping. Leather thimbles allow more flexibility as you push the needle through the fabric. You may need to try different ones to find which type works best.

Straight Pins — Choose long, sharp, thin dressmaker pins with small glass heads. Some quilters like to use pins with flower-shaped heads because they are easy to see and to grasp.

Thread — General-purpose cotton or cotton wrapped thread. Most projects can be pieced using a neutral color such as medium gray or tan.

Embroidery scissors — Small sharp scissors for clipping threads.

MACHINE PIECING

Sewing machine – A sewing machine that produces a good, even, straight stitch is all that is necessary for most piecing and quilting. Make sure machine is in good working order and the tension is set correctly. Use 70 to 90 or 10 to 14 universal (sharp-pointed) machine needles.

Thread – See Hand Piecing.

Straight Pins – See Hand Piecing.

Embroidery Scissors – See Hand Piecing.

Seam ripper – A good quality seam ripper with a sharp point will make the job of removing those occasional mistakes much easier.

MACHINE QUILTING

Sewing machine – See Machine Piecing.

Thread – Use 100% cotton or cotton wrapped thread (not quilting thread) in a neutral or a color that blends with the background fabric for low contrast quilting. If you want your quilting to really stand out, choose a color that contrasts with the background.

Safety Pins – Size 1 or 2 rustproof safety pins are used to pin baste quilt layers together. Some quilters find that curved basting pins, specially designed for quilting, are quick and easy to use.

Embroidery scissors – See Hand Piecing.

Seam ripper – See Machine Piecing.

HAND QUILTING

Needles — Needles for hand quilting are called "betweens". You can purchase them in multi-size packages. You may find it easier to begin with a size 8 then switch to a smaller size 10 or 12 as your skills improve.

Thimble — See Hand Piecing. In addition to a thimble for your sewing hand, some quilters like to wear a thimble or thimble pad on the underneath hand.

Straight Pins — See Hand Piecing.

Thread — Use 100% cotton or cotton wrapped quilting thread in a neutral or a color that blends with the background fabric for low contrast quilting. If you want your quilting to really stand out, choose a color that contrasts with the background.

Embroidery scissors — See Hand Piecing.

Hoop — Designed to hold the 3 layers (quilt top, batting, and backing) together while you quilt. Choose a 12", 14", or 18" hoop for greatest control and portability.

THE GREAT FABRIC QUEST!

SELECTING FABRICS

Selecting your fabrics is an exciting step when making a quilt. Look for fabrics and colors you really like and would enjoy working with. Audition your fabric choices by laying out the bolts or fabric pieces. Stand back about 5 feet and see if any stand out, fade away or look out of place. If they do, replace that fabric with another until you are pleased with the look. If you are unsure if the fabrics you select will work well with each other, a friend or store employee often will have some good suggestions.

Here are a few tips for selecting fabrics:

- Choose good quality medium-weight 100% cotton fabrics. Avoid fabrics that are loosely woven or stretchy. Cotton fabrics are easy to sew and seam allowances will stay flat when pressed.

- Yardage requirements listed for each project are based on 45" wide fabric. After washing and trimming off the selvages, actual usable width is usually 42". Our recommended yardages include this shrinkage, but it never hurts to buy a little extra.

- Some fabric shops and quilt stores sell "fat quarters" which are 18" x 22" (46 cm x 56 cm) cuts of fabric. These are great when you only need a small amount of a certain color.

- Selecting fabric colors can be lots of fun. One simple way to choose fabrics is to pick a print with several colors then find solids or other prints which will coordinate with your main fabric. Remember to include light and dark fabrics.

- Make your quilt sparkle by using fabrics with high contrast. This can be achieved through fabric color (example: using red and white) or fabric characteristics (example: design and size of prints).

- Vary the scale of your prints. A quilt is much more interesting when you use small, medium and large scale prints. Plaids and stripes will add movement, while tone-on-tone prints will add texture.

PREPARING FABRICS

We recommend that all fabrics be washed, dried, and pressed before cutting.

1. To check colorfastness before washing, cut a small piece of the fabric and place in a glass of hot water with a little detergent. Leave the fabric in the water for a few minutes. Remove the fabric from the water and blot with white paper towels. If any color bleeds onto the towels, wash the fabric separately with warm water and detergent, then rinse until the water runs clear. If fabric continues to bleed, choose another fabric.

2. Unfold yardage and separate fabrics by color. To help reduce raveling, use scissors to snip a small triangle from each corner of your fabric pieces. Machine wash fabrics in warm water with a small amount of mild laundry detergent. Do not use fabric softener. Rinse well and then dry fabrics in the dryer.

3. To make ironing easier, remove fabrics from dryer while they are slightly damp. Refold each fabric lengthwise (as it was on the bolt) with wrong sides together and matching selvages. If necessary, adjust slightly at selvages so that fold lays flat. Press each fabric using a steam iron set on "Cotton."

Cutting

SHARP OBJECTS AHEAD!

Before cutting your fabrics, you will need to first decide whether to use templates or to rotary cut. Accuracy in making and using templates or while rotary cutting is a very important step in quiltmaking. Relax and take your time while cutting.

TEMPLATE CUTTING

Making Templates

Templates can be used for either hand or machine piecing. Whether you plan to sew your quilt together by hand or machine will affect the way you make your templates. Our piecing patterns have 2 lines, the inner dashed line is used when making templates for hand piecing and the outer solid line is used when making templates for machine piecing.

1. Lay a piece of template plastic over the pattern. Securing the plastic to the page with removable tape makes tracing easier.

2. If you plan to **hand piece**, use a fine-point marker to trace over the **inner dashed** line, using a ruler to aid in drawing straight lines.

3. If you plan to **machine piece**, use a fine-point marker to trace over the **outer solid** line, using a ruler to aid in drawing straight lines.

4. Trace any pattern markings such as grainline arrows.

5. Use utility scissors to cut out the template on the drawn line.

6. Check your template against the original pattern for accuracy.

Using Templates

1. Follow **Preparing Fabrics**, page 11, to wash, dry, and press fabrics.

2. Place a sheet of extra-fine sandpaper under your fabric to prevent it from slipping while drawing around templates.

3. Place template face down on wrong side of fabric, lining up any grainline arrows with the straight grain of the fabric.

4. Hold your fabric marking pencil at a slight angle against the template to prevent skipping when drawing.

5. For **hand piecing**, draw around template. This is your sewing line. Leaving at least ½" between drawn shapes for the seam allowance, repeat number of times indicated in project instructions for each template (**Fig. 2**). Use scissors to cut out fabric pieces ¼" outside the drawn line.

Fig. 2

6. For **machine piecing**, draw around template. This is your cutting line. Referring to **Fig. 3**, line up edge of template with previously drawn piece and draw around template. Repeat number of times indicated in project instructions for each template. Transfer all pattern markings to fabric. Use scissors to cut out fabric pieces exactly on the drawn line.

Fig. 3

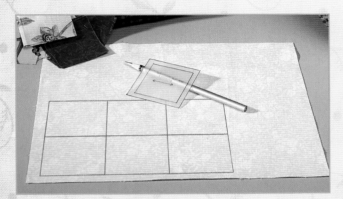

ROTARY CUTTING

Rotary cutting and machine piecing are usually used together because you do not have to mark stitching lines when machine piecing. You can rotary cut pieces for hand piecing, but you will have to draw your stitching line on the fabric ¼" inside the cut edge of each piece.

1. Follow **Preparing Fabrics**, page 11, to wash, dry, and press fabrics.

2. All strips are cut from the selvage-to-selvage width of the fabric unless otherwise indicated in project instructions. Place fabric on the cutting mat, as shown in **Fig. 4**, with the fold of the fabric toward you. To straighten the uneven fabric edge, make the first "squaring up" cut by placing the right edge of your 24" ruler over the left raw edge of the fabric. Place a square or triangular ruler, with the lower edge carefully aligned with the folded edge of the fabric against the right edge of your 24" ruler (**Fig. 4**). Holding the ruler firmly with your left hand, place your little finger off the left edge to anchor the ruler; remove the square ruler. Using a smooth downward motion, make the cut by running the blade of the rotary cutter firmly along the right edge of the ruler (**Fig. 5**). **Always** cut in a direction **away** from your body.

Fig. 4   **Fig. 5**

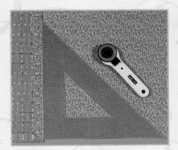   

TIP: Drawing straight lines, which intersect at the corners, will produce a more accurate shape than trying to draw around the corners of a template.

3. To cut each of the strips required for a project, place the ruler over the cut edge of the fabric, aligning desired marking on the ruler with the cut edge (**Fig. 6**); make the cut. When cutting several strips from a single piece of fabric, it may be necessary to occasionally re-square the edge as shown in Step 2.

Fig. 6

4. To square up selvage ends of a strip before cutting pieces, refer to **Fig. 7** and place folded strip on mat with selvage ends to your right. Aligning a horizontal marking on ruler with 1 long edge of strip, use rotary cutter to trim selvage to make end of strip square and even (**Fig. 7**). Turn strip (or entire mat) so that cut end is to your left before making subsequent cuts.

Fig. 7

5. Pieces such as rectangles and squares can now be cut from strips. Usually strips remain folded, and pieces are cut in pairs after ends of strips are squared up. To cut squares or rectangles from a strip, place ruler over left end of strip, aligning desired marking on ruler with cut end of strip. To ensure perfectly square cuts, align a horizontal marking on ruler with 1 long edge of strip (**Fig. 8**) before making the cut.

Fig. 8

6. To cut 2 triangles from a square, cut square the size indicated in the project instructions. Cut square once diagonally to make 2 triangles (**Fig. 9**).

Fig. 9

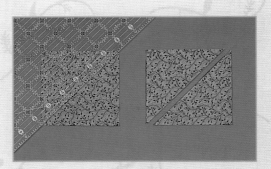

7. Long borders for large quilts are often cut along the more stable lengthwise grain to minimize wavy edges caused by stretching. To remove selvages before cutting lengthwise strips, place fabric on mat with selvages to your left and squared-up end at bottom of mat. Placing ruler over selvage and using squared-up edge instead of fold, follow Step 2 to cut away selvages as you did raw edges (**Fig. 10**). After making a cut the length of the mat, move the next section of fabric to be cut onto the mat. Repeat until you have removed selvages from required length of fabric.

8. After removing selvages, place ruler over left edge of fabric, aligning desired marking on ruler with cut edge of fabric. Make cuts as in Step 3. After each cut, move next section of fabric onto mat as in Step 7.

Fig. 10

TIP: "Measure twice — Cut once."

TIP: Observe safety precautions when using a rotary cutter, since it is extremely sharp. If your rotary cutter has a manual retractable blade, immediately retract the blade after each cut.

Piecing & Pressing

READY, SET, SEW!

Your next decision will be whether to hand or machine piece. The order of piecing follows the same basic steps whether you are sewing by hand or machine. The pieces are sewn into units, the units are sewn into rows, and the rows into a block. The blocks are sewn into rows, and then into a quilt top.

HAND PIECING

Hand piecing uses a running stitch which is formed by weaving the needle and thread through the fabric layers from front to back. Don't be too concerned about stitch length (approximately 6-10 stitches per inch) as you begin; concentrate on making evenly spaced, straight stitches.

Making the Units and Rows

1. Thread a sharps needle with a length of neutral colored general-purpose thread; make a small knot at one end.

2. Place the right sides of the first 2 fabric pieces together. With lighter colored fabric on top, insert a pin through both fabric layers at the beginning and end of drawn seamline (**Fig. 11**). Check that pins come out exactly on drawn line on underneath piece; adjust if necessary. Pin layers together at center and along seamline as needed (**Fig. 12**).

Fig. 11

Fig. 12

3. To begin piecing, insert your needle through both layers of fabric at beginning of seam and take a stitch. Reinsert your needle at the beginning of the seam and take a backstitch (**Fig. 13**).

Fig. 13

4. Load 3-6 running stitches onto your needle then pull thread through fabric (**Fig. 14**). To reinforce the seam, take a backstitch approximately every $3/4$" - 1" (**Fig. 15**). Check the underneath side as you sew to be sure stitches remain even and straight on drawn line.

Fig. 14

Fig. 15

5. Do not sew across or into the seam allowances. At the end of the seam, take a backstitch, make a knot close to the surface and clip thread (**Fig. 16**).

Fig. 16

6. Continue adding pieces until unit or row is completed. Press seam allowances toward darker fabric.

Joining Units or Rows

1. Place the right sides of 2 patchwork units or rows together. Keeping seams aligned and seam allowances free, pin layers together at seam intersections (**Fig. 17**).

Fig. 17

2. Refer to Steps 3 and 4, page 16, to begin piecing.

3. When you reach a seam allowance, take a backstitch just before the seam allowance. Insert needle under the seam allowance and come out on the other side (**Fig. 18**). Take a backstitch close to the seam allowance (**Fig. 19**). At the end of the seam, take a backstitch, make a knot close to the surface and clip thread.

Fig. 18

Fig. 19

4. Press seam allowances toward darker fabric (**Fig. 20**).

Fig. 20

5. Continue adding rows until Block is completed (**Fig. 21**).

Fig. 21

MACHINE PIECING

For good results, it is essential to stitch with an accurate ¼" seam allowance. Presser feet that are exactly ¼" wide are available for most sewing machines. The measurement from the needle to the outer edge of your presser foot may be ¼". If this is the case with your machine, your presser foot is your best guide. If not, measure ¼" from the needle (a ruler or a piece of graph paper with a ¼" grid makes a handy measuring tool) and mark the throat plate with a piece of masking tape (**Fig. 22**).

Fig. 22

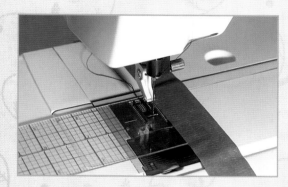

1. Set sewing machine stitch length for approximately 11 stitches per inch. Use a new, sharp needle suited for medium-weight woven fabric.

2. Thread your machine and fill the bobbin with a neutral-colored general-purpose sewing thread (not quilting thread). Stitch on a scrap of fabric to check upper and bobbin thread tension; make any adjustments necessary. Practice stitching on scrap fabric until you are comfortable sewing straight, precise seams.

3. Place the first 2 pieces of your block with right sides together and raw edges matching; pin if desired (**Fig. 23**). (If using pins, remove the pins just before they reach the sewing machine needle.)

Fig. 23

4. Holding the top and bobbin threads out of the way, sew the seam from edge to edge of your fabric (**Fig. 24**). (Some quilters like to begin on a scrap of fabric to prevent puckers or skipped stitches.) It is not necessary to backstitch at the beginning or end of any seam that will be intersected by another seam.

Fig. 24

5. Guide (not push) the fabric under the presser foot. Allow your machine to "feed" the fabric through.

6. Continue adding pieces until unit or row is completed.

7. To sew the rows into blocks, place right sides together and match seams, making sure seam allowances are pressed in the opposite directions; pin if desired (**Fig. 25**). Sew from edge to edge across intersections.

8. Continue adding rows until block is completed (**Fig. 26**).

Fig. 25

Fig. 26

Trimming Seam Allowances

When piecing, some seam allowances may extend beyond the edges of the sewn pieces. Trim away "dog ears" that extend beyond the edges of the sewn pieces (**Fig. 27**).

Fig. 27

PRESSING

Pressing differs from ironing in that you do not slide the iron back and forth across the fabric. To press, lift the iron from one section to the next to avoid stretching or distorting the fabric. Planning your pressing is very important. Most seam allowances are pressed to one side, usually toward the darker fabric. If machine piecing, press the seam allowances as you sew. If hand piecing, press when you complete a section or block. When joining rows, be sure seam allowances are pressed in opposite directions to reduce bulk (**Fig. 28**).

Fig. 28

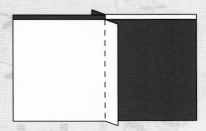

BORDERS

Cutting lengths given for borders in this book include an extra 2" of length at each end for "insurance".

Adding Squared Borders

1. Mark the center of each edge of quilt top.

2. Most of the quilts in this book have the side borders added first. To add side borders, measure across center of quilt top to determine length of borders (**Fig. 29**). Trim side borders to the determined length.

Fig. 29

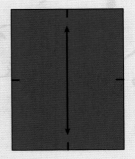

3. Mark center of 1 long edge of side border. Matching right sides, center marks and raw edges, pin border to quilt top, easing in any fullness; stitch. Repeat for other side border.

4. Measure center of quilt top, including attached borders, to determine length of top and bottom borders. Trim top and bottom borders to the determined length. Repeat Step 3 to add borders to quilt top (**Fig. 30**).

Fig. 30

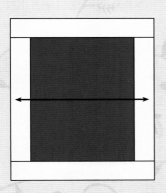

LET'S QUILT A "SANDWICH"

Your last decision is how to quilt your project. Quilting holds the 3 layers (top, batting, and backing) of the quilt together and can be done by hand or machine. Hand quilting produces a softer, antiqued look, but is very time consuming. Machine quilting is much faster and produces tighter stitches. Because marking, layering, and quilting are interrelated and may be done in different orders depending on circumstances, please read the entire **Quilting** section, pages 22 - 25, before beginning the quilting process on your project.

TYPES OF QUILTING
In the Ditch Quilting

Quilting along seamlines or along edges of appliquéd pieces is called "in the ditch" quilting **(Fig. 31)**. This type of quilting should be done on side opposite seam allowance and does not have to be marked.

Fig. 31

Motif Quilting

Quilting a design, such as a feathered wreath, is called "motif" quilting **(Fig. 32)**. This type of quilting should be marked before basting quilt layers together.

Fig. 32

Outline Quilting

Quilting approximately 1/4" from a seam or appliqué is called "outline" quilting **(Fig. 33)**. Outline quilting may be marked, or you may place 1/4"w masking tape along seamlines and quilt along the opposite edge of the tape. (Do not leave tape on quilt longer than necessary, since it may leave an adhesive residue.)

Fig. 33

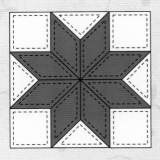

MARKING QUILTING LINES

Fabric marking pencils, various types of chalk markers, and fabric marking pens with inks that disappear with exposure to air or water are readily available and work well for different applications. Lead pencils work well on light-color fabrics, but marks may be difficult to remove. White pencils work well on dark-color fabrics, and silver pencils show up well on many colors. Since chalk rubs off easily, it's a good choice if you are marking as you quilt. Fabric marking pens make more durable and visible markings, but the marks should be carefully removed according to manufacturer's instructions. Press down only as hard as necessary to make a visible line.

When you choose to mark your quilt, whether before or after the layers are basted together, is also a factor in deciding which marking tool to use. If you mark with chalk or a chalk pencil, handling the quilt during basting may rub off the markings. Intricate or ornamental designs may not be practical to mark as you quilt; mark these designs before basting using a more durable marker.

To choose marking tools, take all these factors into consideration and test different markers on scrap fabric until you find the one that gives the desired result.

Choosing and Preparing the Backing

To allow for slight shifting of the quilt top during quilting, the backing should be approximately 4" larger on all sides than quilt top. Yardage requirements listed for quilt backings are calculated for 45"w fabric. Backing for most quilts in this book can be cut from a single width of fabric. To piece backing, if needed, use the following instructions.

1. Measure length and width of quilt top; add 8" to each measurement.

2. Cut backing fabric into 2 lengths slightly longer than the determined length measurement. Trim selvages. Place lengths with right sides facing and sew long edges together, forming a tube (**Fig. 34**). Match seams and press along 1 fold (**Fig. 35**). Cut along pressed fold to form a single piece (**Fig. 36**).

Fig. 34

Fig. 35

Fig. 36

3. Trim backing to correct size, if necessary, and press seam allowances open.

Choosing and Preparing the Batting

Choosing the right batting will make your quilting job easier. The projects in this book are made using cotton batting which does not require tight quilting. If machine quilting, choose a low-loft all cotton or a cotton/polyester blend batting because the cotton helps "grip" the layers of the quilt. For hand quilting, choose a low-loft batting in any of the fiber types described here.

Batting options include cotton/polyester batting, which combines the best of both polyester and cotton battings; fusible battings which do not need to be basted before quilting; bonded polyester which is treated with a protective coating to stabilize the fibers and to reduce "bearding," a process in which batting fibers work their way out through the quilt fabrics; and wool and silk battings, which are generally more expensive and usually only dry-cleanable.

Whichever batting you choose, read the manufacturer's instructions closely for any special notes on care or preparation. When you're ready to use your chosen batting in a project, cut batting the same size as the prepared backing.

Assembling the Quilt

1. Examine wrong side of quilt top closely; trim any seam allowances and clip any threads that may show through the front of the quilt. Press quilt top.

2. If quilt top is to be marked before layering, mark quilting lines (see **Marking Quilting Lines**, page 22).

3. Place backing wrong side up on a flat surface. Use masking tape to adhere edges of backing to surface. Place batting on top of backing fabric. Smooth batting gently, being careful not to stretch or tear. Center quilt top right side up on batting.

4. If **hand quilting**, begin in the center and work toward the outer edges to hand baste all layers together. Use long stitches and place basting lines approximately 4" apart (**Fig. 37**). Smooth fullness or wrinkles toward outer edges.

Fig. 37

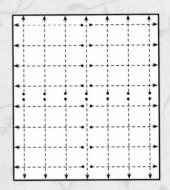

5. When **machine quilting**, use 1" rustproof safety pins to "pin-baste" all layers together, spacing pins approximately 4" apart. Begin at the center and work toward the outer edges to secure all layers. If possible, place pins away from areas that will be quilted, although pins may be removed as needed when quilting.

HAND QUILTING

The quilting stitch is a basic running stitch that forms a broken line on the quilt top and backing. The most important thing to master with hand quilting is keeping your stitches straight and equal in length.

1. Secure center of quilt in hoop or frame. Check quilt top and backing to make sure they are smooth. To help prevent puckers, always begin quilting in the center of the quilt and work toward the outside edges. Some quilters prefer to work without a hoop. You may want to try it both ways to see which is more comfortable for you.

2. Thread needle with an 18"-20" length of quilting thread; knot 1 end.

3. Because you do not want knots to show on the top or bottom surface of your quilt, quilters use a technique called "popping" the knot. Using a thimble, insert needle into quilt top and batting approximately $\frac{1}{2}$" from where you wish to begin quilting. Bring needle up at the point where you wish to begin (**Fig. 38**); when knot catches on quilt top, give thread a quick, short pull to "pop" knot through fabric into batting (**Fig. 39**).

Fig. 38

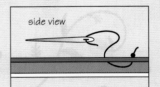

Fig. 39

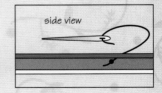

TIP: When machine quilting, use the same color general-purpose thread in the needle and bobbin to avoid "dots" of bobbin thread being pulled to the surface.

TIP: When machine quilting, using general-purpose thread in the bobbin (which matches the backing) will add pattern and dimension to the quilt back without adding contrasting color.

4. Holding the needle with your sewing hand and placing your other hand underneath the quilt, use thimble to push the tip of the needle down through all layers. As soon as needle touches your finger underneath, use that finger to push the tip of the needle only back up through the layers to top of quilt. (The amount of the needle showing above the fabric determines the length of the quilting stitch.) Referring to **Fig. 40**, rock the needle up and down, taking 2 - 3 stitches before bringing the needle and thread completely through the layers. Check the back of the quilt to make sure stitches are going through all layers. With experience, you will be able to load 3-6 or more stitches on your needle before pulling it through the quilt.

Fig. 40

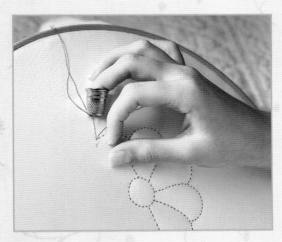

5. When quilting through a seam allowance or quilting a curve or corner, you may need to make 1 stitch at a time.

6. When you reach the end of your thread, knot thread close to the fabric and "pop" knot into batting; clip thread close to fabric.

7. Stop and move your hoop as often as necessary. You do not have to tie a knot every time you move your hoop; you may leave the thread dangling and pick it up again when you return to that part of the quilt.

8. Remove basting threads when quilting is completed.

MACHINE QUILTING
Straight-Line Machine Quilting

The following instructions require a walking foot or even-feed foot. The term "straight-line" is somewhat deceptive, since curves (especially gentle ones) as well as straight lines can be stitched with this technique.

1. Set the stitch length for 6 - 10 stitches per inch and attach the walking foot to sewing machine.

2. After pin-basting, decide which section of the quilt will have the longest continuous quilting line, oftentimes the area from center top to center bottom. Leaving the area exposed where you will place your first line of quilting, roll up each edge of the quilt to help reduce the bulk, keeping fabrics smooth. Smaller projects may not need to be rolled.

3. Start stitching at beginning of longest quilting line, using very short stitches for the first 1/4" to "lock" beginning of quilting line. Stitch across project, using one hand on each side of the walking foot to slightly spread the fabric and to guide the fabric through the machine. Lock stitches at end of quilting line.

4. Continue machine quilting, stitching longer quilting lines first to stabilize the quilt before moving on to other areas (**Fig. 41**).

Fig. 41

5. Remove basting pins when quilting is completed.

Binding

THE FINISH IS NEAR!

MAKING STRAIGHT-GRAIN BINDING

Binding, the last step in the quiltmaking process, encloses the raw edges of your quilt. Binding strips may be cut from the straight lengthwise or crosswise grain of the fabric. Straight-grain binding works well for projects with straight edges, small projects and to accentuate fabric designs such as stripes.

1. Cut lengthwise or crosswise strips of binding fabric the width and length called for in the project instructions. With right sides together, sew the short ends of the strips together to achieve the necessary length for continuous binding.

2. Press seams open. Matching wrong sides and raw edges, press binding in half lengthwise.

ATTACHING BINDING WITH MITERED CORNERS

1. Press 1 end of binding diagonally (**Fig. 42**).

Fig. 42

2. Beginning with pressed end several inches from a corner, lay binding around quilt to make sure that seams in binding will not end up at a corner. Adjust placement if necessary. Matching raw edges of binding to raw edge of quilt top, pin binding to right side of quilt along 1 edge.

3. When you reach the first corner, mark ¼" from corner of quilt top (**Fig. 43**).

Fig. 43

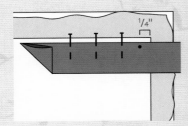

4. Using a ¼" seam allowance, sew binding to quilt, backstitching at beginning of stitching and when you reach the mark (**Fig. 44**). Lift needle out of fabric and clip thread.

Fig. 44

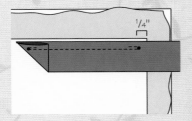

5. Fold binding as shown in **Figs. 45** and **46** and pin binding to adjacent side, matching raw edges. When you reach the next corner, mark ¼" from edge of quilt top.

Fig. 45

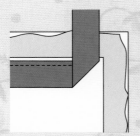

Fig. 46

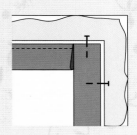

6. Backstitching at edge of quilt top, sew pinned binding to quilt (**Fig. 47**); backstitch when you reach the next mark. Lift needle out of fabric and clip thread.

Fig. 47

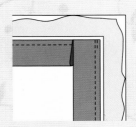

7. Repeat Steps 5 and 6 to continue sewing binding to quilt until binding overlaps beginning end by approximately 2". Trim excess binding.

8. Follow **Making a Hanging Sleeve**, page 28, if desired.

9. Trim backing and batting even with edges of quilt top.

10. On 1 edge of quilt, fold binding over to quilt backing and pin pressed edge in place, covering stitching line (**Fig. 48**). On adjacent side, fold binding over, forming a mitered corner (**Fig. 49**). Repeat to pin remainder of binding in place.

Fig. 48   **Fig. 49**

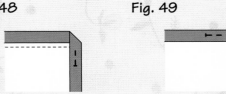

11. Blindstitch binding to backing, taking care not to stitch through to front of quilt (**Fig. 50**).

Fig. 50

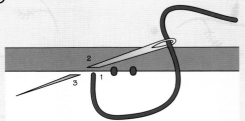

Finishing Touches

JUMP FOR JOY!

MAKING A HANGING SLEEVE

Attaching a hanging sleeve to the back of your wall hanging or quilt before the binding is added allows you to display your completed project on a wall.

1. Measure the width of the wall hanging top and subtract 1". Cut a piece of fabric 7"w by the determined measurement.

2. Press short edges of fabric piece 1/4" to wrong side; press edges 1/4" to wrong side again and machine stitch in place.

3. Matching wrong sides, fold piece in half lengthwise to form a tube.

4. Follow project instructions to sew binding to quilt top and to trim backing and batting. Before blind stitching binding to backing, match raw edges and stitch hanging sleeve to center top edge on back of wall hanging.

5. Finish binding wall hanging, treating the hanging sleeve as part of the backing.

6. Blind stitch bottom of hanging sleeve to backing, taking care not to stitch through to front of quilt.

TIP: For a quick and easy way to hang your quilt on a wall, a decorative curtain rod makes a great hanger. Simply mount the hanging hardware on the wall, slip the rod through your hanging sleeve and place the rod into the hanger.

TIP: If you have a quilt that you would like to display and it was finished without a hanging sleeve, you can easily add one. Follow Steps 1 and 2 above, then fold the fabric piece in half lengthwise to form a tube. Using a 1/2" seam allowance, sew down the long edge of the tube; turn and press. Blindstitch the top and bottom edges of the hanging sleeve to the quilt backing. Now you are ready to hang the quilt.

SIGNING AND DATING YOUR QUILT

A completed quilt is a work of art and should be signed and dated. There are many different ways to do this and numerous books on the subject. The label should reflect the style of the quilt, the occasion or person for which it was made, and the quilter's own particular talents. Following are suggestions for recording the history of quilt or adding a sentiment for future generations.

- Embroider the quilter's name, date, and any additional information on the quilt top or backing using embroidery floss. Matching floss, such as cream floss on white border, will leave a subtle record. Bright or contrasting floss will make the information stand out.

- Make a label from muslin and use a permanent marker to write information. Use different colored permanent markers to make the label more decorative. Hand stitch the label to the back of the quilt.

- Use photo-transfer paper to add an image to a white or cream fabric label. Hand stitch the label to the back of the quilt.

- Piece an extra block from the quilt top pattern to use as a label. Add information with a permanent fabric pen. Hand stitch the block to the back of the quilt.

- For a complete history of your quilt, include on your label who made the quilt, where it was made, when it was completed, the occasion or person it was made for. You could even leave space for future generations to add information about how and when they acquired the quilt.

- For a fun look for your label, use bright colored fabric crayons to color your design.

- For a quick decorative finish, try sewing lace trim or rickrack around the edges or add buttons to the corners of your label.

NINE-PATCH BLOCK

Our first project is a single Nine-Patch Block. It is made up of 9 fabric squares arranged in 3 rows of 3 squares each.

FINISHED BLOCK: 9" x 9" (23 cm x 23 cm)
FINISHED QUILT: 9³/4" x 9³/4" (25 cm x 25 cm)

TIP: If you have a stash of fabric scraps you would like to use for this project, follow the measurements given as inches for the sizes of scraps needed.

THE GREAT FABRIC QUEST!

Refer to **Selecting Fabrics,** *page 10, before beginning your project. You will need to choose 2 contrasting fabrics for your block. We have used a blue tone-on-tone stripe for our dark fabric and a small-scale yellow print for our light fabric. Yardage requirements are based on 45" (114 cm) wide fabric.*

> ¹/8 yd (11 cm) or a 10" x 25" (25 cm x 64 cm) rectangle of dark fabric
> ¹/8 yd (11 cm) or a 5" x 16" (13 cm x 41 cm) rectangle of light fabric
> ¹/2 yd (46 cm) or a 15" x 15" (38 cm x 38 cm) square of backing fabric
> ¹/2 yd (46 cm) or a 13" x 13" (33 cm x 33 cm) square of batting

Be sure to follow **Preparing Fabrics,** *page 11, before cutting into those beautiful fabrics.*

SHARP OBJECTS AHEAD!

Now that you have your fabrics selected and prepared, you are ready to cut out the squares. Depending on your chosen cutting method either follow **Template Cutting,** *page 12, or* **Rotary Cutting,** *page 13, to cut fabric. The template pattern is on page 33.*

From dark fabric:
- Cut 5 **squares** 3¹/2" x 3¹/2" (template **A**).
- Cut 2 **binding strips** 2" x 24".

From light fabric:
- Cut 4 **squares** 3¹/2" x 3¹/2" (template **A**).

From backing fabric:
- Cut 1 **square** 13" x 13".

Still have all your fingers? Great! You will need them for the next step – piecing.

Nine-Patch Block (make 1)

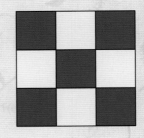

TIP: *Remember to check for consistent $\frac{1}{4}$" seam allowances and accurate unit sizes as you sew. Make any adjustments needed each time you measure.*

READY, SET, SEW!

*Next you will sew the pieces together to make your quilt top. Depending on your chosen sewing method either follow **Hand Piecing**, page 16, or **Machine Piecing**, page 19, to assemble the quilt top. Refer to photo, page 31, and **Unit Diagrams** for fabric placement.*

1. Sew 1 light and 2 dark **A squares** together to make **Unit 1**. Repeat to make a total of 2 **Unit 1's**. At this point, each **Unit 1** should measure $9\frac{1}{2}$" x $3\frac{1}{2}$".

2. Sew 1 dark and 2 light **A squares** together to make **Unit 2**. At this point, **Unit 2** should measure $9\frac{1}{2}$" x $3\frac{1}{2}$".

3. Sew **Units 1** and **2** together to make the **Nine-Patch Block.** At this point, your block should measure $9\frac{1}{2}$" x $9\frac{1}{2}$".

Great Job! You have finished piecing your block! Next let's make a quilt sandwich.

AFTER THE SANDWICH, THE FINISH IS NEAR!

1. Follow **Quilting**, pages 22-25, to mark and layer ("sandwich") your quilt top, then follow **Hand Quilting**, page 24, or **Machine Quilting**, page 25, to complete the quilting process. Our **Nine-Patch Quilt** is hand quilted with outline quilting ¼" from seamline in each square.

2. If you plan to display your quilt on a wall, you may wish to add a Hanging Sleeve to the back of your quilt. Follow **Making a Hanging Sleeve**, page 28, to make and attach a hanging sleeve to your quilt.

3. Follow **Binding**, page 26, to make and attach the binding to your quilt.

Your 1st project is finished! You are officially a quilter! Now let's move on to Lesson 2.

TIP: ¼" wide masking tape laid along the seamlines provides a handy guide for keeping quilting stitches straight.

TIP: Hang your finished quilt on a wall, drape it over a chair back, use it as a trivet on a table, or use buttons to attach it to a purchased pillow.

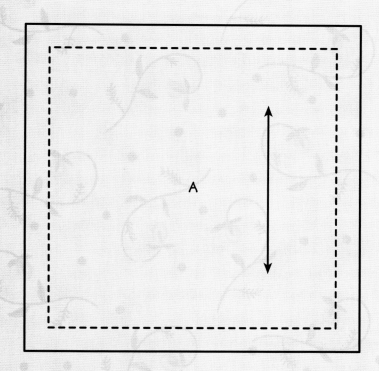

NINE-PATCH TABLE RUNNER

In our second project we join 4 Nine-Patch Blocks together and add a border to make a charming table runner.

FINISHED BLOCK: 9" x 9" (23 cm x 23 cm)
FINISHED QUILT: 42³/₄" x 15³/₄" (109 cm x 40 cm)

TIP: Remember the blade on a rotary cutter is extremely sharp. Retract the blade after every cut!

TIP: Remember to press seams towards darker fabrics when joining squares.

THE GREAT FABRIC QUEST!

Refer to **Selecting Fabrics**, *page 10, for helpful information on choosing your fabrics. You will need 3 different fabrics for your project, a light, a medium, and a dark print. We chose a tan tone-on-tone print for the light, a red plaid for the medium, and a black and red floral for the dark.*

> ¹/₄ yd (23 cm) of light print for Nine-Patch Blocks
> 1⁵/₈ yds (1.5 m) of medium print for Nine-Patch Blocks and backing
> ⁵/₈ yd (57 cm) of dark print for borders and binding
> 46" x 19" (117 cm x 48 cm) rectangle of batting

With your fabrics all selected, follow **Preparing Fabrics**, *page 11, before proceeding.*

SHARP OBJECTS AHEAD!

You are now ready to cut out the pieces. Depending on your chosen cutting method, either follow **Template Cutting**, *page 12, or* **Rotary Cutting,***page 13, to cut fabric. The template pattern is on page 33.*

*See **Piecing Strip Sets**, *page 37, if you would like to try our speedy method for cutting and piecing the* **Nine-Patch Blocks**.

From light print:
- Cut 18 **squares** 3¹/₂" x 3¹/₂" (template **A**).

From medium print:
- Cut 18 **squares** 3¹/₂" x 3¹/₂" (template **A**).
- Cut 1 **backing rectangle** 46" x 19".

From dark print:
- Cut 2 crosswise **side border rectangles** 3¹/₂" x 40¹/₂".
- Cut 2 crosswise **top and bottom border rectangles** 3¹/₂" x 19¹/₂".
- Cut 3 crosswise **binding strips** 2" x 42".

READY, SET, SEW!

Depending on your chosen sewing method either follow **Hand Piecing**, page 16, or **Machine Piecing**, page 19, to assemble the quilt top. Refer to photo, page 35, and **Unit Diagrams** for fabric placement.

1. Sew 1 light and 2 medium **A squares** together to make **Unit 1**. At this point, **Unit 1** should measure 9½" x 3½". Repeat to make a total of 6 **Unit 1's**.

2. Sew 1 medium and 2 light **A squares** together to make **Unit 2**. At this point, **Unit 2** should measure 9½" x 3½". Repeat to make a total of 6 **Unit 2's**.

3. Sew 2 **Unit 1's** and 1 **Unit 2** together to make **Nine-Patch Block No. 1**. Your block should measure 9½" x 9½". Repeat to make a total of 2 **No. 1 Nine Patch Blocks**.

4. Sew 2 **Unit 2's** and 1 **Unit 1** together to make **Nine-Patch Block No. 2**. Your block should measure 9½" x 9½". Repeat to make a total of 2 **No. 2 Nine Patch Blocks**.

5. Alternating **No. 1** and **No. 2 Blocks**, sew **Blocks** together to complete piecing the **Quilt Top Center**. The **Quilt Top Center** should measure 9½" x 36½".

6. Refer to **Borders**, page 21, to add the **borders** to the **Quilt Top Center** .

Unit 1 (make 6)

Unit 2 (make 6)

Nine Patch Block No. 1 (make 2)

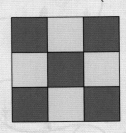

Nine Patch Block No. 2 (make 2)

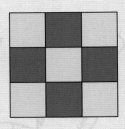

Quilt Top Center

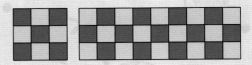

Quilt Top Diagram

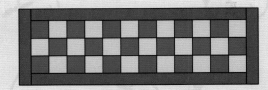

You have now finished piecing the **Quilt Top**! Let's move on to layering, quilting and finishing.

AFTER THE SANDWICH, THE FINISH IS NEAR!

1. Follow **Quilting**, pages 22-25, to mark and layer ("sandwich") your quilt top, then follow **Hand Quilting**, page 24, or **Machine Quilting**, page 25, to complete the quilting process. Our **Nine-Patch Table Runner** is hand quilted with outline quilting ¼" from the seamline in each square and straight-line quilting through the center of each border.

2. Follow **Binding**, page 26, to make and attach the binding to your quilt.

Piecing Strip Sets

Strip sets are made from strips of fabric, usually cut across the width of the fabric, which are sewn together in a specific order. The Strip Sets are then sub-cut to make smaller units, which are used in making the blocks. Using Strip Sets speeds the piecing process by reducing the number of individual pieces you have to cut and sew.

STRIP SETS FOR A NINE-PATCH BLOCK

To speed the cutting and sewing process use this quick Strip Set method. Strips of fabric are cut across the width of the fabric with the Strip width equal to the size of the square called for in the project instructions. For example: If the project instructions call for 3½" squares, cut the strips 3½" wide. The strips are then sewn together (Strip Sets) and sub-cut into smaller units.

1. We used 2 different Strip Sets to make the Nine-Patch Blocks. Strip Set A, made using 2 medium or dark and 1 light strip and Strip Set B made using 2 light and 1 medium or dark strip.

2. You will first need to know how many Strip Sets to make. Divide the usable width of the fabric (42") by the width of the Units (the width of the Units is the same as the width of the squares). For example, 42" divided by 3½" will yield 12 Units per strip.

Strip Set A

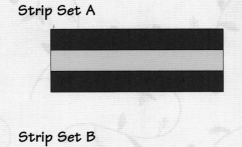

Strip Set B

Unit 1

3½"

Unit 2

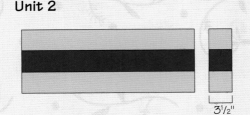

3½"

3. If your project calls for less than 12 Units, you can cut all Units from a single Strip Set. If your project calls for more than 12 Units, divide the total Units needed by the number you can cut from a Strip Set. For example, if you need 20 Units, divide 20 by 12, which will give you 1.6. We round up to the next whole number, so you will have to make 2 Strip Sets.

4. To figure the number of strips you will need to cut, you will need 2 strips of dark and 1 strip of light for each Strip Set A and 1 strip of dark and 2 strips of light for each Strip Set B.

5. Arrange, then sew the strips into **Strip Sets A** and **B**.

6. To make the blocks, cut across the strips at intervals equal to the width of the squares to make **Units 1** and **2**. For example: If the project instructions call for 3½" squares, cut the Units 3½" wide.

7. Arrange the Units as shown in the Block diagram and sew together to make your block. Continue with project instructions to sew Blocks together.

RAIL FENCE QUILT

Our third project, made from four Rail Fence Blocks and a border with contrasting corner squares, is quick and easy to complete.

FINISHED BLOCK: 12" x 12" (30 cm x 30 cm)
FINISHED QUILT: $36^3/4$" x $36^3/4$" (93 cm x 93 cm)

THE GREAT FABRIC QUEST!

Refer to **Selecting Fabrics**, *page 10, before beginning your project. You will need to choose 6 coordinating fabrics for your project. We chose pink and green small, medium, and large-scale prints.*

- $1/4$ yd (23 cm) **each** of 4 different pink or pink and green prints for Rail Fence Blocks
- $1/4$ yd (23 cm) of 1 pink print for corner squares
- 2 yds (1.8 m) of 1 pink print for borders and backing
- $3/8$ yd (34 cm) of 1 green and pink print for binding
- 40" x 40" (102 cm x 102 cm) square of batting

Complete instructions for washing and ironing your fabrics before you cut can be found in **Preparing Fabrics**, *page 11.*

SHARP OBJECTS AHEAD!

Now that you have selected and prepared your fabrics, you are ready to cut out the pieces. Depending on your chosen cutting method, either follow **Template Cutting**, *page 12, or* **Rotary Cutting***, page 13, to cut fabric. Patterns for templates are on pages 54 and 56.*

*See **Strip Sets For A Rail Fence Block**, *page 41, if you would like to try our speedy method for making the Rail Fence Blocks.*

From *each* pink or pink and green print for Rail Fence Blocks:
- Cut 4 **rectangles** $3^1/2$" x $12^1/2$" (template **B**).

From pink print for corner squares:
- Cut 4 **squares** $6^1/2$" x $6^1/2$" (template **C**).

From pink print for borders and backing:
- Cut 4 lengthwise **border rectangles** $6^1/2$" x $24^1/2$".
- Cut 1 **backing square** 42" x 42".

From pink and green print for binding:
- Cut 4 crosswise **binding strips** $2^1/2$" x 42".

READY, SET, SEW!

Now you will sew the pieces together to make your quilt top. Depending on your chosen sewing method either follow **Hand Piecing**, page 16, or **Machine Piecing**, page 19, to assemble the quilt top. Refer to photo, page 39, and **Block Diagram** for fabric placement.

1. Sew 4 rectangles (**B**) together to make a **Rail Fence Block.** Your block should measure 12½" x 12½". Repeat to make a total of 4 **Rail Fence Blocks.**

2. Sew the 4 **Blocks** together to make the **Quilt Top Center.** Your **Quilt Top Center** should measure 24½" x 24½".

3. Sew 1 **corner square** (C) to each end of the **top** and **bottom borders.**

4. Sew **side**, then **top** and **bottom borders** to Quilt Top Center.

You have now finished piecing the **Quilt Top**! Doesn't it look great? Your next step will take you to **Quilting**!

AFTER THE SANDWICH, THE FINISH IS NEAR!

1. Follow **Quilting**, pages 22-25, to mark and layer ("sandwich") your quilt top, then follow **Hand Quilting**, page 24, or **Machine Quilting**, page 25, to complete the quilting process. Our **Rail Fence Quilt** is machine quilted with outline quilting around and straight-line quilting through the center of each "rail", border, and corner square.

2. If you plan to display your quilt on a wall, you may wish to add a Hanging Sleeve to the back of your quilt. Follow **Making a Hanging Sleeve**, page 28, to make and attach a hanging sleeve to your quilt.

3. Follow **Binding**, page 26, to make and attach the binding to your quilt.

Rail Fence Block

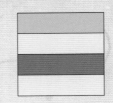

Quilt Top Center

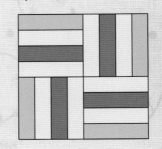

Border

Quilt Top Diagram

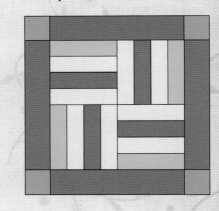

1. When cutting strips for strip sets, cut the strips across the width of the fabric. Strip width is equal to the height of the rectangle called for in the project instructions. For example: if the project instructions call for $3\frac{1}{2}$" x $12\frac{1}{2}$" rectangles, cut the strips $3\frac{1}{2}$" wide.

2. To figure the number of strips you will need to cut, divide the width of the fabric (42") by the length of the rectangles. For example, 42" divided by $12\frac{1}{2}$" will yield 3 rectangles per strip. You will need to cut 2 strips of each fabric to make 4 blocks.

3. Referring to the project photo and diagram for fabric placement, arrange the strips into Strip Sets.

4. Sew the strips together into pairs, then sew the pairs together to form the strip set. To help avoid distortion, sew 1 seam in 1 direction and then sew the next seam in the opposite direction to complete the **Strip Set**.

5. Cut across the Strip Sets at intervals equal to the width of the Block. For example: if the project instructions call for a $12\frac{1}{2}$" block, cut the Strip Sets into $12\frac{1}{2}$" wide units. You can cut 3 units from first strip set and 1 unit from the second strip set. Continue with project instructions to sew Blocks together.

Strip Set

Block

$12\frac{1}{2}$"

TIP: When rotary cutting strips, remember to check that the horizontal line of your ruler aligns with the fold in your fabric and that the vertical line of your ruler aligns with the cut edge of your fabric.

TIP: After the 1st cut, unfold the strip and check that it is perfectly straight. If there is a "V" in the strip, your ruler was not correctly aligned with the fabric. Re-square the crosswise edge before cutting additional strips.

NINE-PATCH WALL HANGING

Our fourth project uses Nine-Patch Blocks and setting squares in an alternating setting. The addition of a double border adds a finishing touch to this attractive wall hanging.

FINISHED BLOCK: 9" x 9" (23 cm x 23 cm)
FINISHED QUILT: 37³/₄" x 37³/₄" (96 cm x 96 cm)

THE GREAT FABRIC QUEST!

Unsure of which fabrics to use? Our **Selecting Fabrics** *section, page 10, is full of hints and tips to guide you. For our wall hanging, we chose a tan tone-on-tone print, a blue medium-scale print, a blue large-scale print, and a red small-scale print.*

- ¹/₂ yd (46 cm) of tan tone-on-tone print for Nine-Patch Blocks and setting squares
- ³/₈ yd (34 cm) of blue medium-scale print for Nine-Patch Blocks
- ⁵/₈ yd (57 cm) of blue large-scale print for outer borders
- ⁵/₈ yd (57 cm) of red small-scale print for inner borders and binding
- 1¹/₄ yds (1.1 m) of backing fabric
- 41" x 41" (104 cm x 104 cm) square of batting

Before cutting your fabrics, be sure to follow **Preparing Fabrics***, page 11.*

SHARP OBJECTS AHEAD!

You are now ready to cut out the pieces. Depending on your chosen cutting method, either follow **Template Cutting***, page 12, or* **Rotary Cutting***,* page 13, to cut fabric. Patterns for templates are on pages 33, 55, and 56.*

*See **Piecing Strip Sets***, page 37, if you would like to try our speedy method for cutting and piecing the* **Nine-Patch Blocks***.*

From tan tone-on-tone print:
- Cut 20 **squares** 3¹/₂" x 3¹/₂" (template **A**).
- Cut 4 **setting squares** 9¹/₂" x 9¹/₂" (template **D**).

From blue medium-scale print:
- Cut 25 **squares** 3¹/₂" x 3¹/₂" (template **A**).

From blue large-scale print:
- Cut 4 crosswise **outer border rectangles** 4¹/₂" x 33¹/₂".

From red small-scale print:
- Cut 2 crosswise **side inner border rectangles** 1¹/₂" x 31¹/₂".
- Cut 2 crosswise **top** and **bottom inner border rectangles** 1¹/₂" x 33¹/₂".
- Cut 4 **corner squares** 4¹/₂" x 4¹/₂" (template **E**).
- Cut 4 crosswise **binding strips** 2" x 42".

From backing fabric:
- Cut 1 crosswise **backing rectangle** 41" x 41".

TIP: To help keep pieces organized, lay out your squares in the order they will be sewn together. Pick up the pieces you will be sewing, sew seam, and return sewn pieces to their place.

READY, SET, SEW!

Depending on your chosen sewing method either follow **Hand Piecing**, page 16, or **Machine Piecing**, page 19, to assemble the quilt top. Refer to photo, page 43, and **Unit Diagrams** for fabric placement.

1. Sew 1 tan and 2 blue **A squares** together to make **Unit 1**. At this point, **Unit 1** should measure 9¹/₂" x 3¹/₂". Repeat to make a total of 10 **Unit 1's**.

2. Sew 1 blue and 2 tan **A squares** together to make **Unit 2**. At this point, **Unit 2** should measure 9¹/₂" x 3¹/₂". Repeat to make a total of 5 **Unit 2's**.

3. Sew 2 **Unit 1's** and 1 **Unit 2** together to make a **Nine-Patch Block.** Your block should measure 9¹/₂" x 9¹/₂". Repeat to make a total of 5 **Nine-Patch Blocks.**

4. Sew **Nine-Patch Blocks** and **setting squares** into **Rows.** Sew **Rows** together to make **Quilt Top Center.** The **Quilt Top Center** should measure 27¹/₂" x 27¹/₂".

5. Refer to **Borders**, page 21, to sew **inner borders** to the quilt top center. After adding the inner borders, measure the **Quilt Top Center**; trim **outer borders** to correct size.

6. Sew 1 **corner square** (E) to each end of the **top** and **bottom borders**.

7. Sew **side**, then **top** and **bottom outer borders** to Quilt Top Center.

With the piecing completed, let's layer, quilt and finish!

Unit 1 (make 10)

Unit 2 (make 5)

Nine Patch Block (make 5)

Quilt Top Center

Border

AFTER THE SANDWICH, THE FINISH IS NEAR!

1. Follow **Quilting**, pages 22-25, to mark and layer ("sandwich") your quilt top, then follow **Hand Quilting**, page 24, or **Machine Quilting**, page 25, to complete the quilting process. Our quilt is hand outline quilted ¹/₄" from the seamlines in each square of the Nine-Patch Blocks, the setting squares and outer borders. There is an "X" quilted through the center of each setting square.

2. If you plan to display your quilt on a wall, you may wish to add a Hanging Sleeve to the back of your quilt. Follow **Making a Hanging Sleeve**, page 28, to make and attach a hanging sleeve to your quilt.

3. Follow **Binding**, page 26, to make and attach the binding to your quilt.

FRIENDSHIP STAR TABLE RUNNER

Our fifth project, made from 4 Friendship Star Blocks, introduces you to working with triangles while making an elegant table runner.

FINISHED BLOCK: 9" x 9" (23 cm x 23 cm)
FINISHED QUILT: 42³/₄" x 15³/₄" (109 cm x 40 cm)

TIP: Remember grain line when positioning a template. The right angle edges of a triangle should be on the straight grain of the fabric.

TIP: Placing a sheet of extra-fine sand paper under your fabric squares will help prevent fabric from shifting while drawing around templates.

THE GREAT FABRIC QUEST!

Refer to **Selecting Fabrics**, page 10, before beginning your project. For our main fabric we chose a large-scale green floral, then used a coordinating medium-scale cream print for the background and a small-scale purple print for the stars.

³/₈ yd (34 cm) of cream print for blocks
1³/₄ yds (1.6 m) of purple print for blocks and backing
⁵/₈ yd (57 cm) of green floral for borders and binding
46" x 19" (117 cm x 48 cm) rectangle of batting

Refer to **Preparing Fabrics**, page 11, before cutting your fabrics.

SHARP OBJECTS AHEAD!

Now that you have selected and prepared your fabrics, you are ready to cut out the pieces. Depending on your chosen cutting method, either follow **Template Cutting**, page 12, or **Rotary Cutting***, page 13, to cut fabric. Patterns for templates are on pages 33 and 56.

*See **Making Triangle-Squares**, page 49, if you would like to try our speedy method for making the Triangle-Squares.

From cream print:
- Cut 16 **squares** 3¹/₂" x 3¹/₂" (template **A**).
- For triangle-squares, cut 16 **triangles** (template **F**) or if **rotary cutting**, cut 8 squares 3⁷/₈" x 3⁷/₈". Cut each square in half once diagonally to make 16 **triangles**.

From purple print:
- Cut 4 **squares** 3¹/₂" x 3¹/₂" (template **A**).
- For triangle-squares, cut 16 **triangles** (template **F**) or if rotary cutting, cut 8 squares 3⁷/₈" x 3⁷/₈". Cut each square in half once diagonally to make 16 **triangles**.
- Cut 1 **backing rectangle** 44" x 19".

From green floral:
- Cut 2 crosswise **side border rectangles** 3¹/₂" x 40¹/₂".
- Cut 2 crosswise **top and bottom border rectangles** 3¹/₂" x 19¹/₂".
- Cut 3 crosswise **binding strips** 2" x 42".

READY, SET, SEW!

Now you will sew the pieces together to make your quilt top. Depending on your chosen sewing method either follow **Hand Piecing**, page 16, or **Machine Piecing**, page 19, to assemble the quilt top. Refer to photo, page 47, and **Diagrams** for fabric placement.

1. Matching long edges, sew 1 cream and 1 purple **triangle** (F) together to make a **Triangle-Square**. Your **Triangle-Square** should measure 3¹/₂" x 3¹/₂". Repeat to make a total of 16 **Triangle-Squares**.

2. Sew 2 **A squares** and 1 **Triangle-Square** together to make **Unit 1**. At this point, **Unit 1** should measure 3¹/₂" x 9¹/₂". Repeat to make a total of 8 **Unit 1's**.

3. Sew 1 **A square** and 2 **Triangle-Squares** together to make **Unit 2**. At this point, **Unit 2** should measure 3¹/₂" x 9¹/₂". Repeat to make a total of 4 **Unit 2's**.

4. Sew 2 **Unit 1's** and 1 **Unit 2** together to make the **Friendship Star Block**. Your block should measure 9¹/₂" x 9¹/₂". Repeat to make a total of 4 **Friendship Star Blocks**.

5. Sew **Blocks** together to complete piecing the **Quilt Top Center**. The **Quilt Top Center** should measure 9¹/₂" x 36¹/₂".

6. Refer to **Borders**, page 21, and **Quilt Top Diagram**, to add the **borders** to the **Quilt Top Center**.

You have finished piecing the Quilt Top! Now let's make a "sandwich" and quilt.

Triangle-Square (make 16)

Unit 1 (make 8)

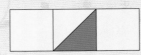

Unit 2

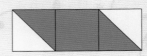

Friendship Star Block

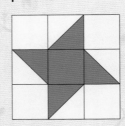

Quilt Top Center

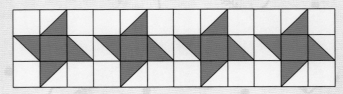

Quilt Top Diagram

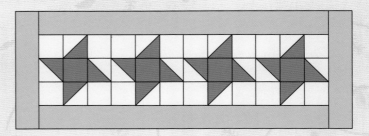

AFTER THE SANDWICH, THE FINISH IS NEAR!

1. Follow **Quilting**, pages 22-25, to mark and layer ("sandwich") your quilt top, then follow **Hand Quilting**, page 24, or **Machine Quilting**, page 25, to complete the quilting process. Our **Friendship Star Quilt** is hand quilted with outline quilting ¹/₄" from the seamline in each square and triangle. There is a straight line quilted through the center of each border.

2. Follow **Binding**, page 26, to make and attach the binding to your quilt.

This technique allows you to make Triangle-Squares without having to handle bias edges.

1. Using one dark square and one light square cut for triangle-squares, place squares right sides together.

2. With the light square on top, draw a diagonal line across the square.

3. Sew seam exactly 1/4" on either side of drawn line (**Fig. 1**).

4. Cut triangles apart on drawn line (**Fig. 2**). Carefully press triangle-squares open (**Fig. 3**), pressing seam allowance toward darker fabric.

5. Trim off "dog ears" that extend beyond the edges of the sewn pieces (**Fig. 4**).

Fig. 1

Fig. 2

Fig. 3

Fig. 4

TIP: When squares are cut in half diagonally, the resulting 45º triangles are often referred to as half-square triangles (HST).

Lesson 6

VARIABLE STAR QUILT

In our sixth project large Triangle-Squares are joined together to make a cheerful Variable Star wall hanging.

FINISHED BLOCK: 9" x 9" (23 cm x 23 cm)
FINISHED QUILT: 48³/₄" x 48³/₄" (124 cm x 124 cm)

TIP: If you have not tried rotary cutting and machine piecing but would like to, this is a great project to use those techniques.

THE GREAT FABRIC QUEST!

*Refer to **Selecting Fabrics**, page 10, for suggestions about fabrics to use in your project. While the scale of the prints we chose for our wall hanging does not vary greatly, the high contrast of soft yellows and crisp blues makes a bold statement.*

3⁷/₈ yds (3.5 m) of yellow print No. 1 for background and backing
12" x 24" (30 cm x 61 cm) rectangle of yellow print No. 2 for star center square
³/₈ yd (34 cm) of light blue print No. 1 for star center and border corners
12" x 12" (30 cm x 30 cm) of light blue print No. 2 for star center
³/₈ yd (34 cm) of medium blue print for star points
1¹/₄ yds (1.1 m) of dark blue print for borders and binding
52" x 52" (132 cm x 132 cm) rectangle of batting

*Test for colorfastness, wash, and iron your fabrics before cutting by following **Preparing Fabrics**, page 11.*

SHARP OBJECTS AHEAD!

*Next step – cutting! Depending on your chosen cutting method, either follow **Template Cutting**, page 12, or **Rotary Cutting***, page 13, to cut fabric. Patterns for templates are on pages 55 and 56.*

See **Making Triangle-Squares, page 49, if you would like to try our speedy method for making the Triangle-Squares.*

From yellow print No. 1:
- Cut 4 **squares** 9¹/₂" x 9¹/₂" (template **D**).
- Cut 8 **triangles** (template **G**) or if **rotary cutting**, cut 4 **squares** 9⁷/₈" x 9⁷/₈". Cut each square in half once diagonally to make 8 **triangles**.
- Cut 2 **backing rectangles** 27" x 52¹/₂".

From yellow print No. 2:
- Cut 4 **triangles** (template **G**) or if **rotary cutting**, cut 2 **squares** 9⁷/₈" x 9⁷/₈". Cut each square in half once diagonally to make 4 **triangles**.

From light blue print No. 1:
- Cut 2 **triangles** (template **G**) or if **rotary cutting**, cut 1 **square** $9^7/_8$" x $9^7/_8$". Cut each square in half once diagonally to make 2 **triangles**.
- Cut 4 **squares** $6^1/_2$" x $6^1/_2$" (template **C**).

From light blue print No. 2:
- Cut 2 **triangles** (template **G**) or if **rotary cutting**, cut 1 **square** $9^7/_8$" x $9^7/_8$" Cut each square in half once diagonally to make 2 **triangles**.

From medium blue print:
- Cut 8 **triangles** (template **G**) or if **rotary cutting**, cut 4 **squares** $9^7/_8$" x $9^7/_8$". Cut each square in half once diagonally to make 8 **triangles**.

From dark blue print:
- Cut 2 crosswise **side border rectangles** $6^1/_2$" x $36^1/_2$".
- Cut 2 crosswise **top and bottom border rectangles** $6^1/_2$" x $36^1/_2$".
- Cut 5 crosswise **binding strips** 2" x 42".

READY, SET, SEW!

Depending on your chosen sewing method either follow **Hand Piecing**, page 16, or **Machine Piecing**, page 19, to assemble the quilt top. Refer to photo, page 51, and **Diagrams** for fabric placement.

1. Matching long edges, sew 1 yellow No. 1 and 1 medium blue **triangle** (**G**) together to make a **Triangle-Square No. 1**. Your **Triangle-Square** should measure $9^1/_2$" x $9^1/_2$". Repeat to make a total of 8 **No. 1 Triangle-Squares**.

2. Matching long edges, sew 1 yellow No. 2 and 1 light blue No. 1 **triangle** (**G**) together to make a **Triangle-Square No. 2**. Your **Triangle-Square** should measure $9^1/_2$" x $9^1/_2$". Repeat to make a total of 2 **No. 2 Triangle-Squares**.

Triangle-Square No. 1 (make 8)

Triangle-Square No. 2 (make 8)

TIP : The long sides of the Half Square Triangles are bias edges. Handle these edges carefully to avoid stretching or distorting the triangles.

3. Matching long edges, sew 1 yellow No. 2 and 1 light blue No. 2 **triangle (G)** together to make a **Triangle-Square No. 3**. Your **Triangle-Square** should measure 9$\frac{1}{2}$" x 9$\frac{1}{2}$". Repeat to make a total of 2 **No. 3 Triangle-Squares**.

Refer to **Quilt Top Diagram**, for orientation of Triangle-Squares for Rows 1-4.

4. Sew 2 **D squares** and 2 **No. 1 Triangle-Squares** together to make **Rows 1** and **4**. Your **Rows** should measure 9$\frac{1}{2}$" x 36$\frac{1}{2}$".

5. Sew 2 **No. 1 Triangle-Squares**, 1 **No. 2 Triangle-Square** and **1 No. 3 Triangle-Square** together to make **Rows 2** and **3**. Your **Rows** should measure 9$\frac{1}{2}$" x 36$\frac{1}{2}$".

6. Sew the **Rows** together to complete piecing the **Quilt Top Center**. The **Quilt Top Center** should measure 36$\frac{1}{2}$" x 36$\frac{1}{2}$".

7. Sew 1 **corner square (C)** to each end of the **top** and **bottom borders**.

8. Sew **side**, then **top** and **bottom borders** to Quilt Top Center.

The **Quilt Top** is finished! Let's move on to **Quilting** to make it into a finished quilt.

Triangle-Square No. 3 (make 2)

Row 1

Row 4

Row 2

Row 3

Border

Quilt Top Diagram

*TIP: A label sewn onto the back of your quilt allows you to record important information about your quilt. See **Signing and Dating Your Quilt**, page 29, for how to's.*

AFTER THE SANDWICH, THE FINISH IS NEAR!

1. Follow **Quilting**, pages 22-25, to mark and layer ("sandwich") your quilt top, then follow **Hand Quilting**, page 24, or **Machine Quilting**, page 25, to complete the quilting process. Our **Variable Star Quilt** is hand outline quilted $1/4$" and $1^{1}/4$" from the seamline in each square and triangle. There is a straight line quilted through the center of each border and an "X" in each corner square.

2. If you plan to display your quilt on a wall, you may wish to add a Hanging Sleeve to the back of your quilt. Follow **Making a Hanging Sleeve**, page 28, to make and attach a hanging sleeve to your quilt.

3. Follow **Binding**, page 26, to make and attach the binding to your quilt.

To trace $1/2$ patterns with a center fold, lay template plastic over pattern, trace $1/2$ pattern, rotate plastic 180°, lining up center fold line, and trace remaining $1/2$ pattern.

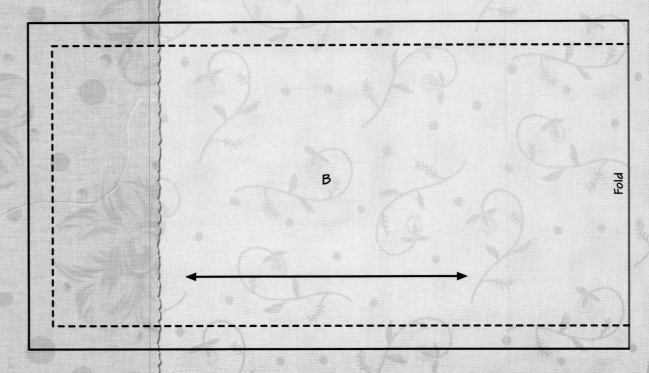

B

Fold

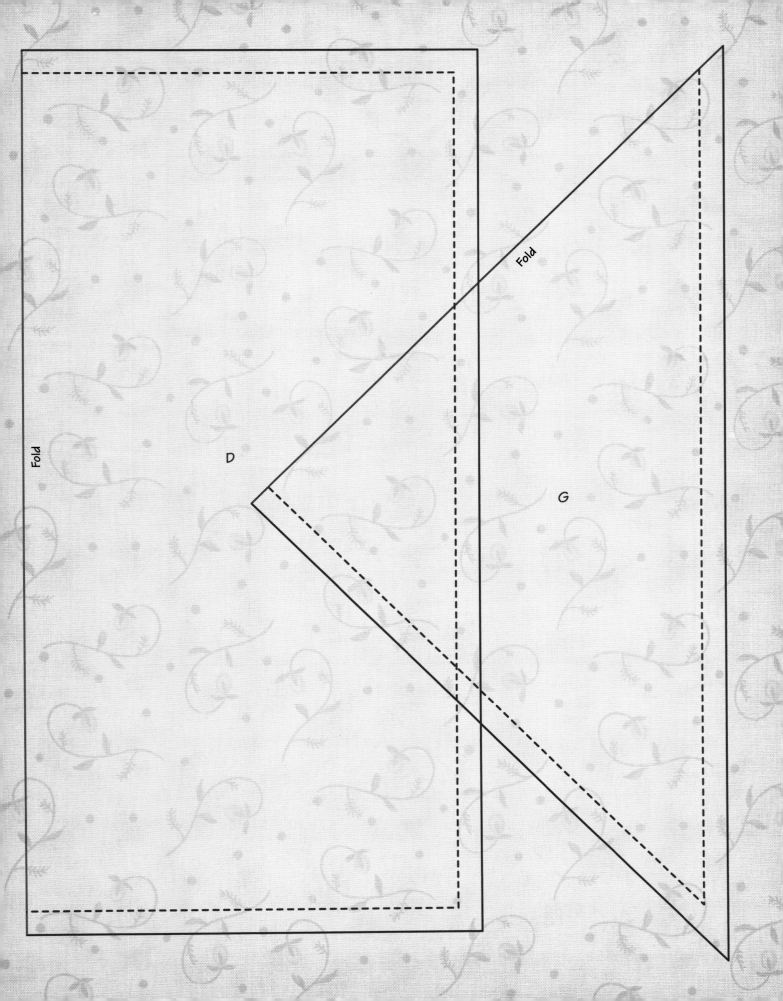

Fold

Fold

D

G

Fold

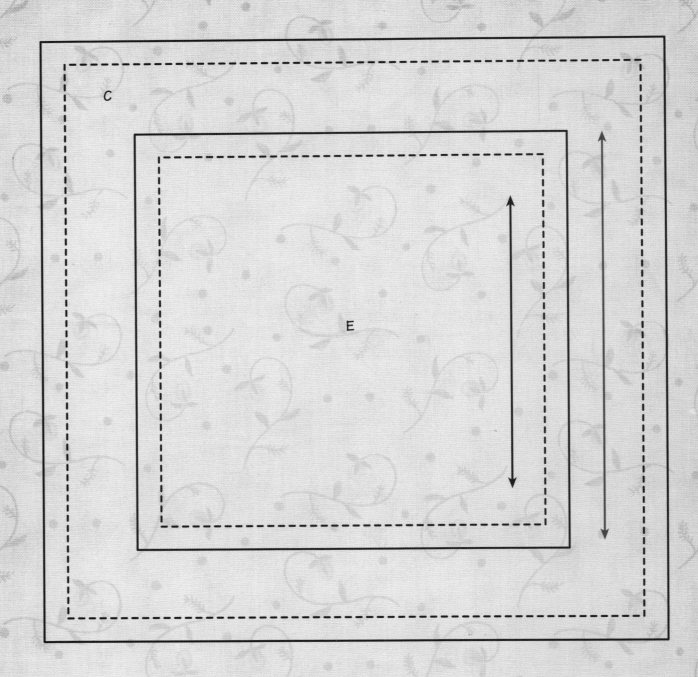

C

E

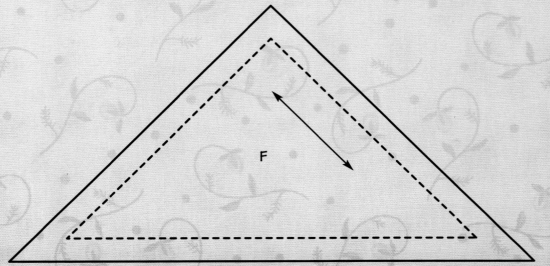

F